The Residency Mirage

The Silent Breath

Meghna Kinjalk

BookLeaf Publishing

India | USA | UK

Dedication

To the hands that heal,
To the soul that endures,
And to the heart that never gives up.
This book is a tribute to every silent breath,
Every sleepless night,
And every moment of compassion that defines the path
of a surgeon.
May these words be a testament to resilience,

And a reminder that poetry, like healing, has the power
to transform.

Preface

The Residency Mirage "The Silent Breath" is a reflection of the residency days of a girl which were lost with every wound closure. The surgical residency had been glorified as a "happy" journey of learning and doing groundbreaking surgeries. Little did she knew about the wounds of sadness, deceit, invisible fears, unspoken lies and silent tears which she had to stitch up myself without any anesthesia. To everyone who is chasing their dreams and ever felt lost, may you find piece of yourself in these pages.

(P.S. -All poems in this book are works of fiction—any resemblance to real persons, places, or institutions is purely coincidental and unintended.)

Acknowledgements

I bow my head in gratitude to God-for giving me the courage to feel and the words to write.

To my father, Dr. Nishindra Kinjalk, and my mother, Mrs. Alka Kinjalk — who stood tall when the world turned away, fueling my dreams with unwavering love and every resource they could muster. To my siblings, Dr. Aarushi Kinjalk and Dr. Tushar Kinjalk — whose quiet strength and constant belief lit the path I walk today.

And to dear friends — thank you for standing beside me, holding space for the chaos and the calm.

I also acknowledge the mentors who became my greatest teachers. They taught me resilience and forced me to find my voice.

"Lastly, to all who believed, doubted, hurt, or healed her — thank you.
In some way or another, you've all found a home in her words."

1. Apron vs Soul

White coats off, moist soul stepped inside
The soul with passion, walks a dream by side.
Though unaware of what lay ahead,
A chaos it is, where we are led.

Soul caresses the sharp scalpel world,
Hopes unrelenting, fears unfurled.
Here peep the doubts, a trembling voice,
Whispers, is this the choice?

2. Break or Bend-Beginning is the end

No reason, sent from operation room to ward,
Hopes of surgery swiftly floored.
A month went by, no cuts, no claims,
Only emergencies, faces and names.

No stepping out, no glimpse of sky,
Just duty calls as days went by.
Eat , work, and sleep where the patients lay,
The hospital walls owned night and day.

What to do next? No answers sent,
Is this the start of the descent?
One month down- beginning or end?
In surgical dreams, we break, we bend.

3. Thirties tragedy

A sacrifice of family, a sacrifice for kin,
A battle outside, a battle within .
Missed the magic a mother weaves,
In silent nights, the heart still grieves.

Missing furious festivals bright,
while duty called her every night.
Weddings passed, no songs, no cheer,
Functions faded year by year.

Only weekends, if luck was kind,
A wedding or two she would sometimes find.
But in this life she chose to live,
It's love and loss she had to give.

4. Troublemaker is the real troubleshooter

Thought of quitting and running away,
Residency felt too tough to stay.
Thoughts were the trouble but they were the cure,
To pursue the dream or not,
She was pretty unsure.

"Survival is difficult in this differently *dominated* field,
Years of hard work will produce no yield."
A teacher told her to quit and start afresh,
"Take a break, you need some rest."

Started meditation, learnt spirituality,
A new dawn with a new reality.
She never gave up and pursued her dreams,
Fueled by hope and guiding beams.

5. PPP - Pause Problem Partnership

Realizing loneliness isn't enough,
The road gets dark, the journey tough.
You need someone to stand beside,
A hand to hold, a place to hide.

Are you good for someone too ?
Is someone good enough for you ?
It takes time, it takes trust,
Patience grows where hearts adjust.

A war with time , with work, with pain,
Fighting hard just to sustain.
Battles with seniors, cold and loud,
Internal wars you are not allowed.

Above it all, the silence grows
In the path of love, the struggle shows.
Pauses come, some stay too long,
Testing if the bond is strong.

Yet somehow , through the endless fight,
You search for love, you chase the light.

6. Money Magic

Money has magic, a glittering charm,
But chasing it steals the heart's warm.
Practicing for money, the soul runs dry,
The joy of healing waves goodbye.

The more you earn, the less you feel,
Family moments you cannot steal.
Magic fades from home and heart,
While chasing wealth, you drift apart.

7. Razor Blade memory

All these thoughts fade away,
When duty calls, there is no delay.
A two year old swallowed a half razor blade,
That night's memory still cannot fade.

Parents anxious, mother in tears,
As a primary surgeon , my plan was clear.
Performed the surgery at two in night,
The blade was shining in the light.

The blade removed from the stomach,
That left us with nothing much.
Had a good night sleep,
And another fear took a leap.

Next morning, mother thanked with a precious smile,
The kind of win, that makes it worthwhile.

8. Corona Year -a different fear

Second year of residency, goals set high
Hoping for surgeries that touch the sky.
Thoughts of breakthrough filled the air,
A chance to prove skill, to truly dare.

But Corona rose from somewhere,
The people were found nowhere.
Only emergencies were to be operated,
The surgeons were all now automated.

Hopes were shattered, dreams were frozen,
Another year - she decided to find her Zen.
Irony hit- for the first time had time,
 The partner search continued,
Ultimately could not find.

People stayed away from people,
We were given rooms in lavish hotels.
What kind of life, what twisted fate,
when dreams and love must sit and wait ?

Almost a year swiftly passed by,
The opportunities were lost, which we could not deny.

9. Our "table" manners

Our table was surrounded by
surgeon, assistant and staff nurse.
This table was different for sure,
A team was needed where trust must pull us through.

Assisting was the new bonding,
Clock was ticking, hands were steady.
Step by step, anesthetist were ready.
Surgery started ,had laser focus on,
Suppressed the hunger and Nature' call
Because *the show must go on!*

A female surgeon, fighting her own battles,
Fighting for space amongst the other *cattle.*
Lost in maze of her own thoughts,
Seniors to please, juniors to teach
And what not?

Learnt few dictums:
Seniors are always right,
No matter what you see in sight.
Cross your line, and consequences you face.
Barred from surgeries,
Then difficult to get back into *the race.*

10. The bracelet lover

Another night, an emergency call,
A baby in pain, too small.
A bracelet swallowed, magnetic and round,
Trapped inside the intestine,
Mother reported when it was nowhere found.

The team prepared for another night,
To search for broken beads,
Another interesting case to *fight*.

Beads scattered, some stuck,
Two pulled apart-now the intestine were stuck.
A stroke of luck, the mother's hand,
The same bracelet helped us understand.

Piece by piece, we removed the beads,
Answered prayers, fulfilled the needs.

Another night over, the chaos subdued,
Morning out patient department duty, the patients
queued.
Half awake, no breakfast in sight,
The day had begun , no end in sight.

Some satisfaction, though utterly drained,
A healer's heart, but the body strained.

11. Midnight coffee and the theft

Midnight rounds , a consultant led,
Taught us resilience , where angels fear to tread.
Through sleepless nights, we learned to strive,
Perseverance kept our hopes alive.

One night, she caught a thief in ward,
His trembling hands and face looked scarred.
The night was still, ward was *cold,*
Another story there, yet left untold.

Police was alerted and consultant called,
After discussions the matter was resolved.

Then coffee shared when rounds were done,
Life and spirit talked till one.
What waits beyond the fleeing stage?
What dreams we will chase beyond this stage?

A journey long, yet worth the fight,
With lessons learned in the dead of night.

12. The Love : A mirage too

They said love blooms in residency,
but all she found was dependency-
On coffee shots and broken sleep,
While feelings sank, not running deep.

Hearts don't race, but pulses do,
For crashing vitals, not "I love you"
In this desert of call and rounds,
Love is just a mirage that never surrounds.

So here she stand - with scalpel pride,
My only date? The spleen inside.

13. Opportunistic night

Night emergency, mass casualty,
An unfinished building fell heavily.
Wailing patients filled the air,
Chaos, pain and deep despair.

No time to rest, gave my best.
Surgeries performed, lives were saved,
Some we pulled back from the grave.

A parent lost, the baby survived,
From ruins and sorrow, a life revived.
A stranger stepped in, heart open wide,
Offered adoption, stood by their side.

In the mayhem, a new family, a new home was found,
Hope rising gently from battleground.
With every heartbeat, whispers of grace,
A flicker of love in this shattered place.

Through blood and tears, the spirit will thrive,
In darkness we gather, together we strive.
For in the wreckage, the human heart beats,
Resilience ignites where despair and hope meet.

16. The breakdown

Some days were bad, some days the worst,
Pushed to limits, felt truly cursed.
A Senior said, "Step past the line,
Forget your morals, you will do just fine."

But she stood firm, did no wrong,
Harmed no patient, stayed strong.

The other one said," She is unfit for the course,
Disobeys commands, shows no remorse."
It broke us down, the hardest hit,
Almost quit- thought that was it.

But family stood, their voices strong,
Pushed her forward where she belongs.
Found her strength, returned with fire,
Fueled by their faith, rising higher.

14. The Hostel cubicle

A small hostel room,
Noodles, pasta, curry to cook.
Home away from home,
But after duty this was her home.

Hardly time to visit or stay,
ten minutes daily- bathe and eat,
Then back to war with tired feet.

Her roommate lived a life apart,
Her nights began as others feel dark.
She would call from bars, half lost, half wild,
"Come get me back," she slurred and smiled.

Confused, ignored, too numb to feel,
Depression crept, its touch too real.
was living or being shoved to breathe?
A ghost of dreams, with none beneath.

15. The clerk, clock and the tea

Had work at college, went on time,
The clerk showed up an hour past nine.
Excuses ready, tales so fine,
And straight to breakfast - "First , let me dine."

An hour later, its lunch again,
Work delayed-Its all in vain.
A little shuffle, a lazy sigh,
"Tea break now, the clock flew by."

The files pile up, the work grows,
Responsibility? They sometimes know.
You plead, beg and find your way,
But never dare disrupt their day.

From duties packed, she carved a slot,
But one full day was still too short.
Phone calls, pleadings, all in vain,
For work they should have done-its insane.

As if life's weight was not enough,
This too piled on-its getting tough.

17. Thesis, Chaos and a Dying sun.

The thesis began before the storm,
With dreams of research taking form.
Sample size- strong, the plan was grand,
Then came a virus, swept the land.

Academics stalled, the world stood still,
Locked in rooms -her *samples*, against their will.
The research waited, pressure grew,
Duties doubled, deadlines too.

And midway through that heavy fight,
The Virus stole her guide one night.
Grief and chaos, another blow,
Two months lost in paper's flow.

A new guide allotted, clock ticking fast,
three months left- how long could her soul last?
Research at peak, the duties burned,
Emergencies came, no lesson learned.

And in those nights, a thought took flight,
Why not run, escape this fight ?
Who cares? One day we will fade away,

Dust on earth- what's left to say?

The printing costs , a cruel surprise,
Crooked system, built on lies.
Empty pockets, debts to pay,
Survival games- no other way.

Tuitions started, juniors came,
She taught, she fought, she played the game.
Earned by bread, survived the phase,
No breather came, just hollow praise.

18. Post exam gifts

Exam season never seemed to end,
Each time they said," A gift, my friend."
"Just this last, endure the test
After this, you will have your rest."

From nursery days to medical halls,
The same old fear forever calls.
Questions out of the syllabus fly,
You sit and wonder- *But why, oh why?"*

"Attempt them all," the elders say,
"Marks will come, just find a way."
One paper done, the next appears,
The cycle spins for endless years.

And so it went, till the post-graduation door,
The same old promise, heard before-
"This is the last, the final race,
After this, you will find your place."

But gifts and peace were never near,
Just newer tests, and the same old fear.

19. Magical dreams

Exams all done- what sweet relief,
No more struggle, no more grief.
The books now dumped,
They have had their fun.

"Now is her time," she proudly say,
Keeping all her worries at bay.
Relations to renew, romance to chase,
soulmate search- "Where is Tinder's place?"

No more "yes sir" no more lists,
Her rules, her way - what a bliss!

This is the life those shows had shown,
She is finally in that zone.
Scrubs on, attitude too,
Except. rent's due- What's new?

Ah well- the dream, it's kind of true,
With a little drama. And bills, too!

20. Degrees, Drinks and Mirage Dance

Months had passed since results were done,
The invite came- "Come join the fun!"
Convocation, cap and pride,
But little did she know what lurked inside.

Registrations first- the endless queues,
Also awaited the missing degrees blues.
The "highest" students last in the grandest show,
Energy was already running low.
No royal celebration, no fancy treat,
Warm mongo juice- What a feat!

Oh poor, the circus spins,
Even *this*- no one wins.

Is this the glory we all pursue?
Convocation- a mirage too !
A comedy staged with gowns and hats,
They call it honor. She calls it "rats!"

21. The Mirage continues ..

After "the" degree, the race's not done,
The chase begins, but nowhere to run.
Shortage screams- no posts in sight,
Vacancies filled in the dead of night.

Favors traded, names arranged,
Dreams once magical, now estranged.

Degree in hand, she roams, she pleads,
Her file of papers-her only creed.

From pillar to post, she chases the air,
The promised future-never there.

Interviews turn- "are you wed?" they pry,
Qualifications lost beneath that sky.

What? Is this the prize we claim?
The struggle is real, the rules- the same.

Stress and hope in the endless ties,
Life, it seems, is built on lies.

She will write it down, the final page,
A simple truth- life is a mirage.

www.ingramcontent.com/pod-product-compliance
Lightning Source LLC
La Vergne TN
LVHW010847200726

843508LV00012B/2788